Let's get Curious

Life Skills for Littles

12 FOUNDATIONAL FOCUS POINTS FOR LITTLE LEARNERS

By Natasha Caballero

Let's Get Curious

Life Skills for Littles

12 FOUNDATIONAL FOCUS POINTS FOR LITTLE LEARNERS

By Natasha Caballero

COPYRIGHT ©2025 NATASHA CABALLERO

PUBLISHED BY: NATASHA CABALLERO LLC
DESIGN BY: NATASHA CABALLERO
CANVA STOCK IMAGES
PHOTOGRAPHS: NATASHA CABALLERO

ALL RIGHTS RESERVED. NO PART OF THIS BOOK MAY BE REPRODUCED, DISTRIBUTED, OR TRANSMITTED IN ANY FORM OR BY ANY MEANS, WITHOUT THE PRIOR WRITTEN PERMISSION OF THE PUBLISHER, EXCEPT IN THE CASE OF BRIEF QUOTATIONS EMBODIED IN CRITICAL REVIEWS AND CERTAIN OTHER NONCOMMERCIAL USES PERMITTED BY COPYRIGHT LAW.

FIRST EDITION
ISBN 979-8-9929108-0-3

DEDICATION

TO MY FAMILY - FOR ALL OF THE
ENCOURAGEMENT AND SUPPORT I HAVE
RECEIVED THROUGHOUT THE YEARS

Table of Contents

12 FOUNDATIONAL FOCUS POINTS FOR LITTLE LEARNERS

INTRO PG.1
1. LETTERS AND PHONICS PG.2
2. NUMBERS AND COUNTING PG.6
3. COLORS AND SHAPES PG.10
4. FINE MOTOR SKILLS PG.14
5. GROSS MOTOR SKILLS PG.18
6. SOCIAL SKILLS PG.22
7. EMOTIONS AND FEELINGS PG.26
8. PERSONAL HYGIENE AND HEALTH PG.30
9. ART AND CREATIVITY PG.34
10. MUSIC AND MOVEMENT PG.38
11. STORYTELLING AND READING PG.42
12. NATURE AND SCIENCE PG.46
OUTRO PG.51
ABOUT ME PG.52

Intro

To the Parents of Littles

THIS BOOK IS FOR PARENTS OF YOUNG CHILDREN WHO WANT TO BE MORE INVOLVED WITH ACTIVE LEARNING BUT DON'T KNOW WHERE TO START

MAY THE IDEAS AND SUGGESTIONS IN THIS BOOK OFFER YOU GUIDANCE AND SUPPORT AS YOU STEWARD THE YOUNG MINDS YOU ARE POURING INTO

Curiosity Corner

Letters & Phonics

- INTRODUCTION TO THE ALPHABET
- LETTER RECOGNITION
- BASIC PHONICS SOUNDS

Learn it

What letter is it?

INTRODUCE THE LETTER
BY ITS NAME

Sound it

What sound
does it make?

EXPLORE THE SOUNDS
THE LETTER MAKES

Write it

How do you make
this letter?

SHOW THE STEPS TO
MAKE THE LETTER

Use it

What words begin
with this letter?

LIST SOME WORDS THAT
START WITH THE LETTER

Let's break it down

Supplies you need:

- ALPHABET LETTERS
- WRITING UTENSIL
- PAPER/WHITE BOARD

Steps to take:

- START ONE LETTER AT A TIME
- INTRODUCE THE LETTER
- SOUND IT, WRITE IT, USE IT
- REPEAT AS NECESSARY

Curiosity Corner

Numbers & Counting

- RECOGNIZING NUMBERS
- COUNTING
- UNDERSTANDING BASIC CONCEPTS OF QUANTITY

Learn it

What number is it?

INTRODUCE THE DIGIT
AND THE WORD

Count it

How much is
the number?

RELATE THE NUMBER
TO ITS QUANTITY

Write it

How do you make
this number?

SHOW THE STEPS TO
MAKE THE NUMBER

Use it

Where do you
see this number?

FIND WAYS TO USE THE
NUMBER AROUND THE ROOM

Let's break it down

Supplies you need:
- NUMBERS(CHART/FLASHCARDS)
- WRITING UTENSILS
- PAPER/WHITE BOARD
- COUNTERS (CRACKERS/CUBES)

Steps to take:
- START IN GROUPS OF FIVE
- INTRODUCE THE NUMBERS
- GRADUALLY BUILD AND ADD ON
- REPEAT AS NECESSARY

Curiosity Corner

Colors & Shapes

- IDENTIFYING & NAMING:
- COLORS
- BASIC GEOMETRIC SHAPES

Learn it

What is it?

IDENTIFY THE
COLOR/SHAPE

Find it

Where do you see
this color/shape?

RECOGNIZE COLORS/SHAPES
AROUND YOU

Draw it

How do use/make
this color/shape?

EXPLORE THE WAYS TO
MAKE THE COLORS/SHAPES

Imagine it

What can you
create with all
colors/shapes?

USE YOUR IMAGINATION
TO CREATE WITH
COLORS/SHAPES

Let's break it down

Supplies you need:

- SHAPE EXAMPLES
- WRITING UTENSIL
- PAPER/WHITE BOARD
- COLORS(PAINT, FOOD COLORING, CRAYONS OR MARKERS)

Steps to take:

- START ONE SHAPE AT A TIME
- START WITH PRIMARY COLORS
- SAY & SHOW FOR EACH NEW SHAPE AND COLOR

Curiosity Corner

Fine Motor Skills
(ACTIVITIES TO DEVELOP HAND-EYE COORDINATION, SUCH AS)

- CUTTING
- DRAWING
- MANIPULATING SMALL OBJECTS

Watch it

What are we doing?

SHOW THE SKILL

Think it

Which body parts are being used?

IDENTIFY WHICH BODY PARTS ARE NEEDED TO DO IT

Copy it

What motions do you do?

IMITATE THE STEPS THAT WERE SHOWN

Try it

How do you put it all together?

REPEAT AND PRACTICE DOING THE SKILL

Let's break it down

Supplies you need:
- OBJECTS RELATED TO SKILL
- SCISSORS/PAPER
- WRITING UTENSIL/PAPER
- CHEERIOS/CONTAINER

Steps to take:
- MODEL SKILL
- TRY DOING IT TOGETHER
- START WITH ONE MOTION AND BUILD AS SKILL INCREASES

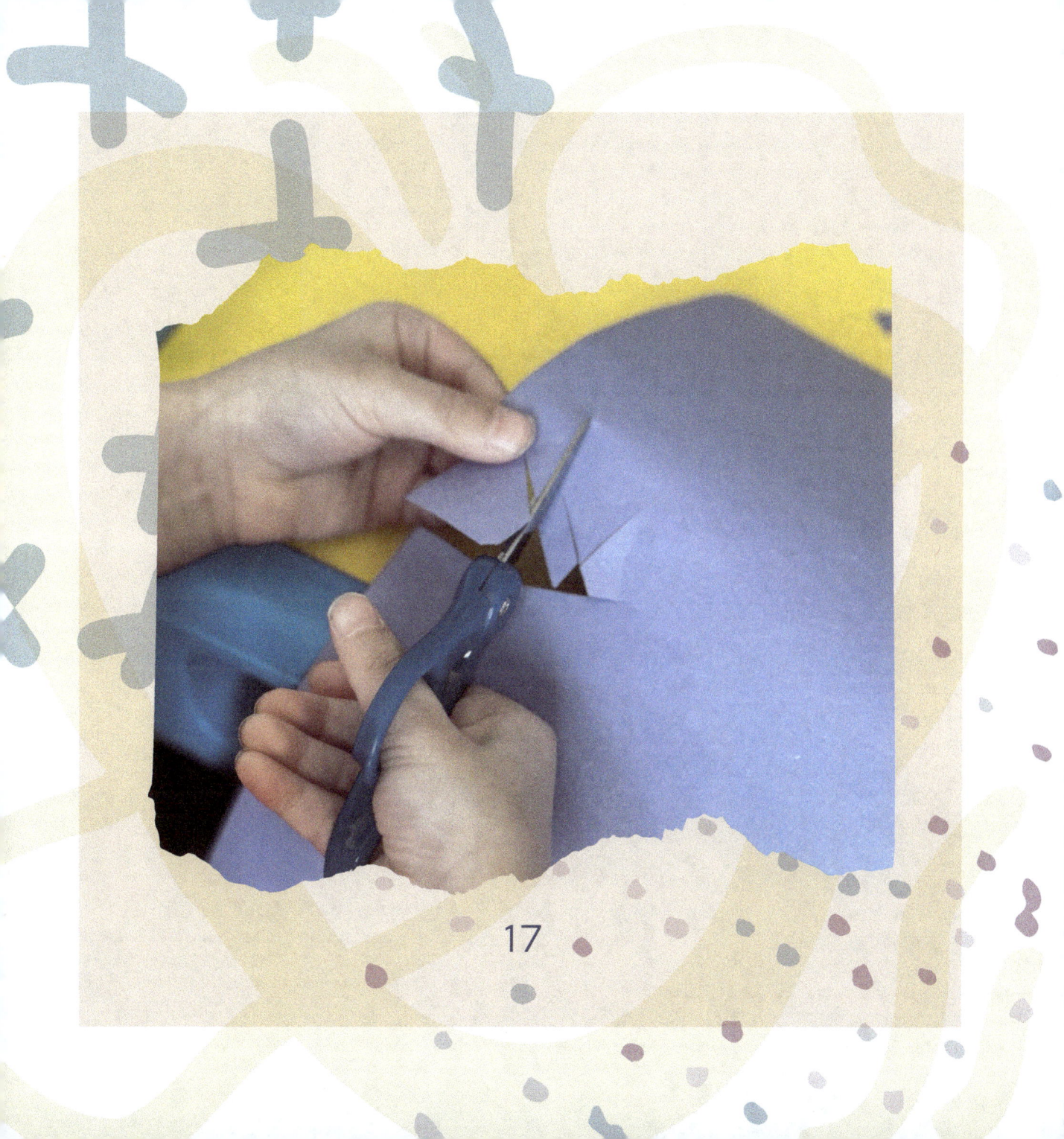

Curiosity Corner

Gross Motor Skills

(PHYSICAL ACTIVITIES TO DEVELOP LARGE MUSCLE GROUPS)

- RUNNING
- JUMPING
- CLIMBING

Watch it

What are we doing?

SHOW THE SKILL

Think it

Which body parts are being used?

IDENTIFY WHICH BODY PARTS ARE NEEDED TO DO IT

Copy it

What motions do you do?

IMITATE THE STEPS THAT WERE SHOWN

Try it

How do you put it all together?

REPEAT AND PRACTICE DOING THE SKILL

Let's break it down

Supplies you need:

- OPTIONAL: GYM EQUIPMENT
- OBSTACLE COURSE CREATION
- PILLOWS/OBJECTS/CHALK

Steps to take:

- CHECK SURROUNDINGS FOR SAFETY
- SAY & SHOW THE SKILL
- GET CREATIVE & HAVE FUN

Curiosity Corner

Social Skills

- LEARNING TO SHARE
- TAKE TURNS
- INTERACT POSITIVELY WITH PEERS AND ADULTS

Watch it

What are we doing?

MODEL THE SOCIAL SKILL

Think it

Why/when do we use this skill?

UNDERSTAND THE PURPOSE

Study it

How do we get better with it?

PRACTICE USING THE SOCIAL SKILL

Observe it

Where are others using this skill?

LOOK AROUND TO NOTICE THE SKILL BETWEEN OTHERS

Let's break it down

Supplies you need:

- OPPORTUNITIES TO DEMONSTRATE SKILL
- OBJECTS RELATED TO SKILL (EX: SHARING)

Steps to take:

- MODEL THE SKILL
- FAMILIARITY AND LEARNING COMES WITH REPETITION AND EXPLANATION

Curiosity Corner

Emotions & Feelings

- RECOGNIZING AND EXPRESSING EMOTIONS
- DEVELOPING EMPATHY
- UNDERSTANDING OTHERS' FEELINGS

Identify it

What are you feeling?

NAME THE EMOTION

Process it

How does this feeling affect you?

NAME YOUR REACTIONS

Release it

What are healthy ways to express?

LEARN HEALTHY WAYS FOR EXPRESSING FEELINGS

Detect it

How can you tell how someone feels?

IDENTIFY WAYS TO OBSERVE HOW OTHERS EXPRESS

Let's break it down

Supplies you need:

- DIFFERENT EMOTION CARDS
- JOURNAL/WRITING UTENSIL

Steps to take:

- NAME & EXPLAIN DIFFERENT EMOTIONS
- USE REAL OPPORTUNITIES TO PAUSE AND BRING EMOTIONAL AWARENESS

Curiosity Corner

Personal Hygiene and Health

- WASHING HANDS
- BRUSHING TEETH
- UNDERSTANDING THE IMPORTANCE OF CLEANLINESS

Watch it

What are we doing?

MODEL THE SKILL

Think it

Why/when do we apply it?

UNDERSTAND THE PURPOSE

Study it

How do we get better doing this?

PRACTICE THIS SKILL

Repeat it

How often do we do this?

TURN THIS SKILL INTO A HABIT/ROUTINE

Let's break it down

Supplies you need:
- OBJECT RELATED TO SKILL (SOAP/TOOTHBRUSH)

Steps to take:
- SAY & SHOW SKILL
- TRY IT TOGETHER
- CREATE A ROUTINE

Curiosity Corner

Art & Creativity

- DRAWING
- PAINTING
- CRAFTING

Imagine it

What are we making?

THINK AND USE YOUR IMAGINATION

Make it

How does it look

DRAW/ MAKE WHAT YOU ARE IMAGINING

Color it

What colors can we use?

GET CREATIVE WITH COLORS AND SUPPLIES

Admire it

How does it look/ make you feel?

TAKE A MOMENT TO ADMIRE YOUR CREATION

Let's break it down

Supplies you need:

- PAPER/WHITE BOARD
- CRAYONS/MARKERS/PAINT
- TABLE
- (CLEAN UP SUPPLIES HANDY)

Steps to take:

- PREP THE AREA AHEAD OF TIME
- ALLOW CREATIVITY TO FLOW
- HAVE SUPPLIES FOR CLEANUP ACCESSIBLE TO MODEL THAT STEP AS WELL
- SHOWCASE CREATION

Curiosity Corner

Music & Movement

- SINGING SONGS
- PLAYING INSTRUMENTS
- MOVING TO MUSIC

Watch it

What are we doing?

SING/SHOW THE SONG/DANCE

Copy it

How do we sing and learn the dance?

TEACH IT IN SMALLER PARTS

Try it

How do we do the entire song?

PUT ALL THE PARTS TOGETHER

Repeat it

How do we remember it?

PRACTICE SINGING AND DANCING AGAIN AND AGAIN

Let's break it down

Supplies you need:
- MUSIC/PLAYLIST
- SOME INSTRUMENTS (OR OBJECTS THAT CAN BE USED AS INSTRUMENTS)

Steps to take:
- PLAY MUSIC
- FAMILIARITY DEVELOPS WITH REPETITION
- HAVE FUN

Curiosity Corner

Storytelling & Reading

- LISTENING TO STORIES
- EXPLORING BOOKS
- FOSTERING A LOVE FOR READING AND STORYTELLING

Show it

What is it?

SHOW THE BOOK, PICTURES AND WORDS

Read it

How does the story go?

READ THE BOOK OUT LOUD

Review it

What was the story about?

REVISIT KEY TOPICS

Share it

What have we learned from it?

SHARE THE STORY AND THE LESSONS

Let's break it down

Supplies you need:
- BOOKS

Steps to take:
- CREATE A STRUCTURE OR ROUTINE
- ALLOW LITTLES TO BE CURIOUS
- ENCOURAGE ANY FORM OF ENGAGEMENT

Curiosity Corner

Nature & Science

- EXPLORING
- SEASONS, WEATHER, PLANTS, ANIMALS
- SIMPLE SCIENCE EXPERIMENTS

Learn it

What is it?

TEACH THE SUBJECT

Observe it

Where do you see it in your day?

MAKE CONNECTIONS

Study it

How does it happen/function?

EXPLAIN HOW IT EXISTS/LIVES

Explore it

Where can you go to study it?

VISIT PLACES TO STUDY IT

Let's break it down

Supplies you need:

- WEATHER CARDS
- BOOKS/PICTURES
- REAL LIFE EXAMPLES (IF POSSIBLE)

Steps to take:

- OBSERVE THE WEATHER
- SHOW EXAMPLES
- INCREASE EXPOSURE TO DIFFERENT WEATHER/ANIMALS

Outro

THERE ARE SO MANY MORE WAYS TO BE INTERACTIVE WITH YOUR LITTLE LEARNERS, BUT IT IS ALSO IMPORTANT TO REMEMBER TO HAVE GRACE WITH YOURSELF IN THESE EARLY YEARS.

MY HOPE IS THAT THIS BOOK PROVIDES THE IDEAS YOU MAY NEED TO HAVE SOME SORT OF GUIDANCE AND STRUCTURE, AS WELL AS SUPPORT AND ACKNOWLEDGEMENT FOR YOU TO DO WHAT IS BEST FOR YOUR FAMILY IN YOUR SEASON.

THANK YOU SO MUCH FOR YOUR SUPPORT - CONNECT WITH ME MORE AT NATASHALUANNACABALLERO@GMAIL.COM

NATASHA CABALLERO LLC IS A CREATIVE HUB FOUNDED BY A PASSIONATE STAY-AT-HOME MOM. WE SPECIALIZE IN MUSIC LESSONS, PHOTOGRAPHY, EVENT PLANNING/DECOR, AND CUSTOMIZED PRODUCTS/PLANNING AND IDEAS FOR PARENTS OF YOUNG CHILDREN.

OUR MISSION IS TO PROVIDE EXCEPTIONAL SERVICES THAT ADD JOY AND CONVENIENCE TO THE LIVES OF PARENTS. WITH A COMMITMENT TO QUALITY AND CREATIVITY, WE STRIVE TO MAKE EVERY MOMENT SPECIAL FOR YOU AND YOUR FAMILY.

FIND MORE AT NATASHACABALLERO.COM

This resource was created to support parents and caregivers in introducing 12 foundational learning focus points to young children in a simple, flexible, and experience-based way. The activities and ideas shared are based on personal experience, creative exploration, and practical routines that have served our own family well.

The content is intended to encourage and inspire—not prescribe—a specific educational approach. Every family is different, and you are encouraged to adapt these suggestions to best support your child's unique needs, pace, and personality.

This resource is not a curriculum and is not meant to replace professional educational, developmental, or medical guidance. It is offered in love and in support of parents seeking to nurture curiosity, connection, and growth in everyday moments.

Review

12 Foundational Focus Points for Little Learners

1

Letters & Phonics

2

Numbers & Counting

3

Colors

&

Shapes

4

Fine Motor Skills

5

Gross Motor Skills

6

Social Skills

7

Emotions & Feelings

8

Personal Hygiene & Health

9

Art & Creativity

10

Music & Movement

11

Storytelling & Reading

12

Nature & Science

www.ingramcontent.com/pod-product-compliance
Lightning Source LLC
Chambersburg PA
CBHW080450100526
44581CB00003B/95